Fruit Water

100 Vitamin Water Recipes

by Barbara O'neill

How to Make Infused Water

We know that water is our life. You can make a lot of combinations of useful wate

It's easy to make. All you need is fresh produce (fruit, vegetables, herbs, spices) a
cool water. Choose what you want. Wash, chop your produce and add to your wate

The amount of produce you use is up to you based on how much water

you're infusing, the more produce you add, the more intense the flavor will be. Th
intensity will also depend on how long you let the ingredients infuse.

Some produce will add flavor immediately, other produce will soak longer.

The end-product should be stored at room temperature for about three hours.
Then put it in the refrigerator.
I recommend peeling the citrus peel because the drink will be bitter.

The fruit water is almost calorie free and gives you a refreshing way to be happy.

You can use water with any number of herbs, spices, fruit and vegetables! And
remember, the longer it sits, the more flavorful the water will be.

Use thin slices or small cubes because the flavor will infuse more quickly.

Let's start!

pineapple   cherry   apple

strawberry   basil

apple

cinnamon

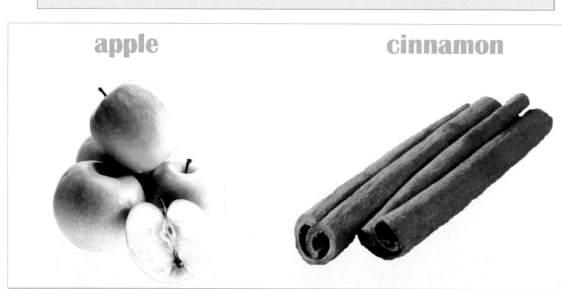

melon

grape

ginger pear lemon

watermelon rosemary

lemon

honey

lime

mint

cherry

lime

honey

mint

ginger

lemon

11

cinnamon   lemon

12

ginger   lemon   mint

13

ginger

lemon

mint

cucumber

14

raspberry

lime

15

cucumber

mint

16

kiwi

mint

17

orange   lime   lemon

18

pineapple   mint

19

dewberry

salvia

20

mint

lime

cucumber

21

strawberry   **basil**   **lemon**

22

orange   **pineapple**   **ginger**

23

orange   mint   lemon

24

mango   cucumber   ginger

25

grape   cucumber   raspberry

26

pomegranate   pineapple   lemon

27

lemon   cucumber   ginger

28

green tea   lime   lemon

29

kiwi   passion fruit   guava

30

kiwi   cherry   pomegranate

31

strawberry **raspberry** **lemon**

32

strawberry **orange** **cranberry**

33

raspberry   apple   blueberry

34

ginger   mint   lemon

cucumber

35

strawberry   **basil**   **raspberry**

36

strawberry   **lemon**

37

mint   apple

38

strawberry   cucumber   basil

39

basil   strawberry   mint

cucumber

40

dewberry   strawberry

mint   cucumber   lemon

mint   cucumber   lemon

thyme   rosemary

43

strawberry   **apple**   **lemon**

44

basil   **cucumber**   **pumpkin**

strawberry **cucumber** **lemon**

mint **blueberry**

strawberry **kiwi** **peach**

47

grape **orange** **red currant**

48

plum **cherry** **peach**

strawberry **kiwi** **apple**

mint **grapefruit** **lemon**

cucumber

51

black currant orange blueberry

52

mint raspberry lime

53

lemon   cinnamon   apple

54

strawberry   raspberry   lemon

mint

55

grapefruit **cucumber** **lemon**

56

strawberry **cucumber** **kiwi**

57

strawberry **rosemary** **watermelon**

58

strawberry **watermelon**

apricot **peach**

59

strawberry　　　**mint**　　　**lime**

cucumber

60

cherry　　　**thyme**　　　**peach**

61

ginger   orange   blueberry

62

apricot   cherry   lime

63

grapefruit · mint

64

melon · cucumber · mint

65

raspberry   ginger   lemon

66

mint   pineapple   lime

67

mint   strawberry   apple

68

tangerine   blueberry

69

watermelon

basil

70

orange

cucumber

lemon

mint

cherry

71

orange   watermelon   apricot

72

watermelon   plum   orange

73

black currant   lavender flowers   blueberry

74

melon   strawberry   lime

cucumber

75

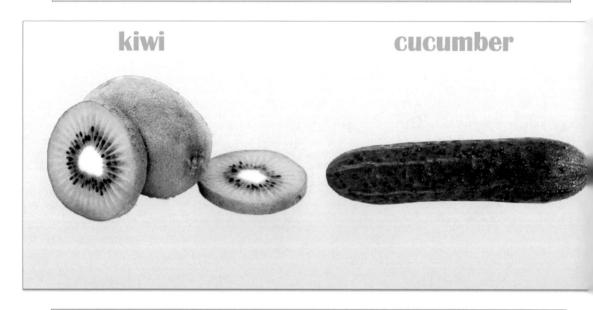

kiwi

cucumber

76

melon

raspberry

lime

watermelon   **coconut milk**

watermelon   **coconut milk**   **peach**

watermelon   **coconut milk**   **pear**

watermelon   **apple**   **pear**

81

apple

coconut milk

82

apple

pear

cinnamon

83

apple **pear** **lemon**

kiwi

84

apple **kiwi** **pumpkin**

85

mint   honey   lime

86

grapefruit   salvia   lemon

87

grapefruit   rosemary   mint

88

mint   lemon   basil

cucumber

plum **lime** **lemon**

plum **pear** **lemon**

tangerine

91

ginger   orange   basil

92

mint   lime   lemon

cucumber

93

grapefruit   cucumber   basil

94

ginger   plum   lemon

95

pomegranate **orange** **strawberry**

96

cranberry **melon** **watermelon**

basil   **banana**   **peach**

dewberry   **raspberry**   **strawberry**

mint

dewberry   **grapefruit**   **strawberry**

cranberry   **plum**   **apple**